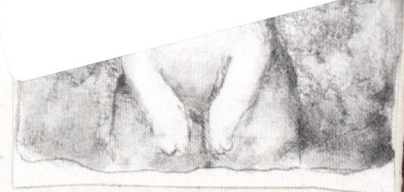

HIGHER GROUND

For Evan - T S

First published in Great Britain 2025
by New Frontier Publishing Europe Ltd
Vicarage House, 58-60 Kensington Church Street, London W8 4DB
www.newfrontierpublishing.co.uk

978-1-915167-76-7 (HB)

Text and illustrations © 2025 Tull Suwannakit
The rights of Tull Suwannakit to be identified as the
author/illustrator of this work have been asserted.
Additional images © Adobe Stock 2025

A CIP catalogue record for this book is available from the British Library.

Edited by Tasha Evans • Designed by Verity Clark

Printed in China

1 3 5 7 9 10 8 6 4 2

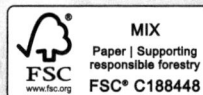

MIX
Paper | Supporting
responsible forestry
FSC
www.fsc.org   FSC® C188448

HIGHER
GROUND

Tull Suwannakit

NEW FRONTIER PUBLISHING

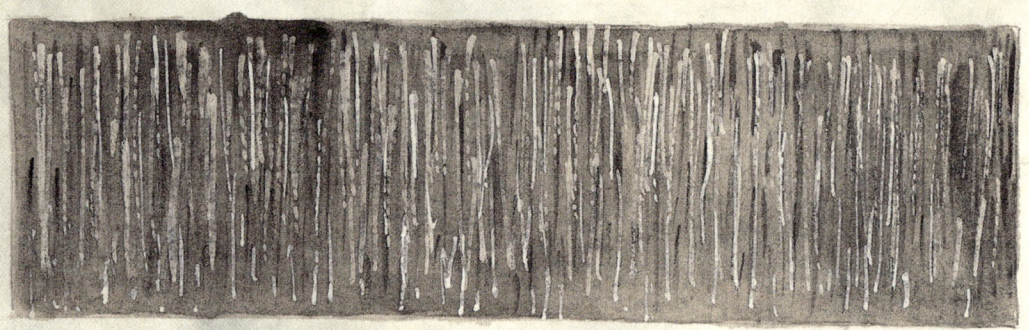

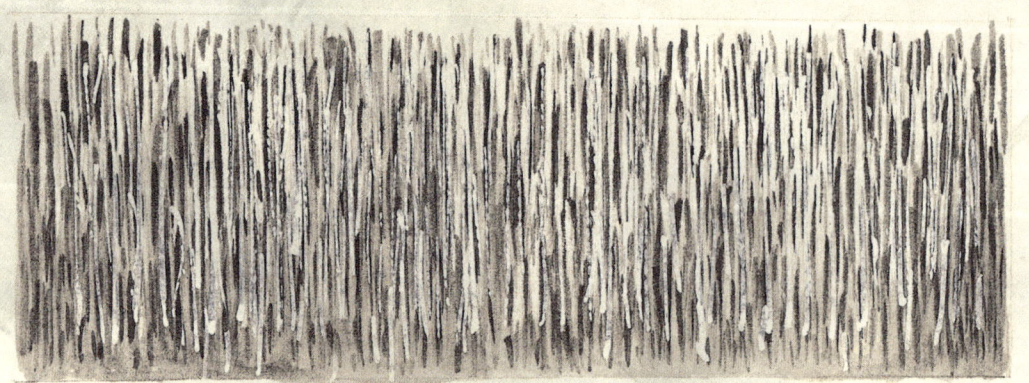

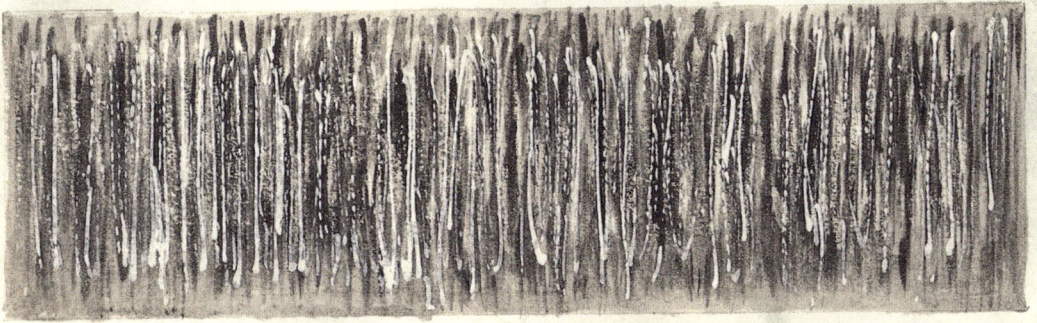

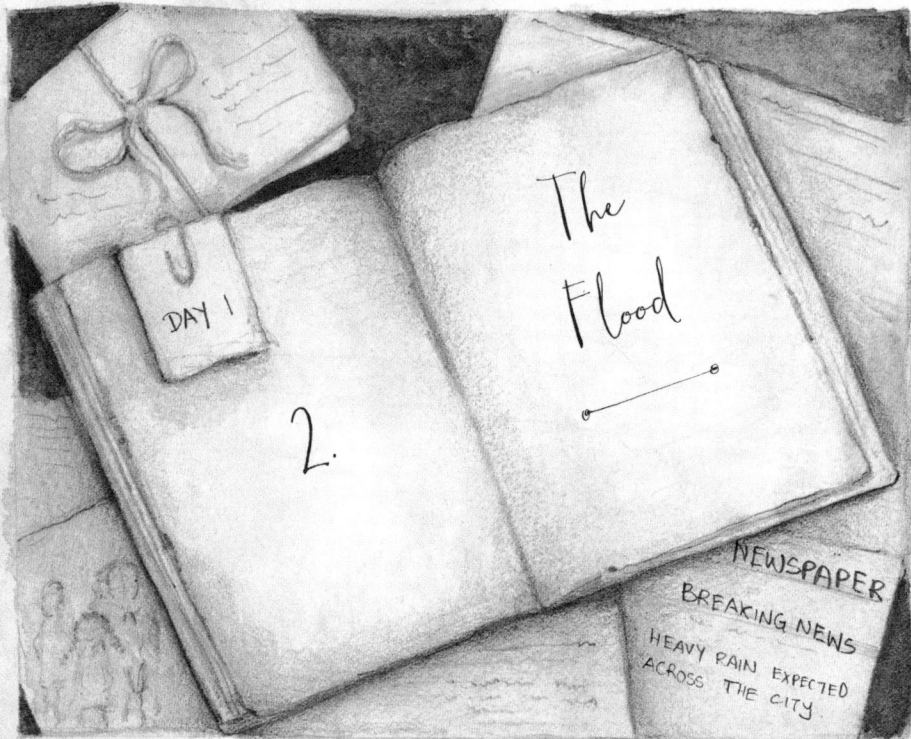

DAY 1

2.

The
Flood

NEWSPAPER
BREAKING NEWS
HEAVY RAIN EXPECTED
ACROSS THE CITY

The Great Flood. That's what Grandma called it.

Nothing could contain the water.

BREAKING NEWS
FLOOD RAVAGES CITY

Not a lake nor a reservoir.

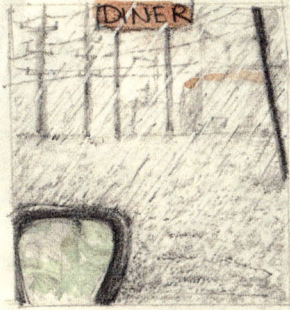

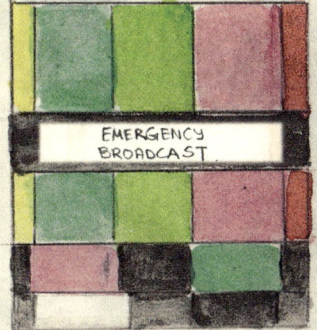

Everyone left the city before the water came.

Everyone but us.

Grandma was frail and weak.

By the time we reached the stairs ...

510 A   512 B

5

the water was lapping at our feet.

It was too late.

We took refuge in the shed as the storm battered on.

Thunder roared out its warning. Lightning struck.

The downpour was ferocious.
It stayed like that all through the night.

My sister and I were scared.
But Grandma held us tight. She kept us safe.

The next morning, everything was quiet.

Stillness. Silence.

From over the garden wall,
we looked to the streets below.

There were no houses, no cars, no street signs.

Buildings and shops had disappeared.
Everything was covered.

Just water. Water all around.

For many days, we waited for help to arrive.

We left a note on the roof.

But help never came.

Days turned into weeks.

Weeks into months.

There was no one. Just us.

'Never lose hope,' Grandma said.

'Life can be meaningful even in the darkest of days.'

3. Lessons Learnt

Every day, Grandma taught my sister
and me all that she knew.

HOW TO TIE A KNOT

5 MOST IMPORTANT THINGS TO SURVIVE AN APOCALYPSE

1. WATER
2. FOOD
3. SHELTER
4. FIRE
5. HOPE

BINDING KNOT IS USEFUL WHEN SECURING AN OBJECT OR MULTIPLE LOOSE OBJECTS TOGETHER.

'RIGHT OVER LEFT, LEFT OVER RIGHT'

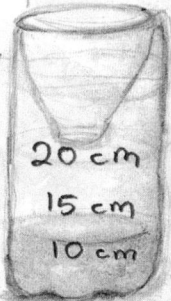

20 cm
15 cm
10 cm

DIY RAIN CATCHER

1. CUT THE BOTTLE IN HALF
2. INSERT THE TOP HALF INTO THE BOTTOM HALF

HOW TO START A FIRE

A BOTTLE FILLED UP WITH WATER CAN BE USED TO START A FIRE BY ADJUSTING THE DISTANCE FROM THE BOTTLE AND TINDER TO FIND WHERE IT CREATES THE BRIGHTEST BEAM FROM THE SUN

Running stitch to repair holes and tears

Little things she said that

RAIN CATCHER USING A PLASTIC SHEET

PLASTIC JUG
THIS TECHNIQUE IS A GREAT WAY OF HARVESTING WATER WHEN RAIN IS EXPECTED, SO THAT WE CAN CONSERVE THE WATER IN THE TOWER.

Fresh water supply from the water tower. On average, the tower can hold 37,854 litres of water. One person uses around 3 litres of water per day. So this means that 9 litres of water is used between the 3 of us. If our calculation is correct, it will take 11 years to use up all the water from the tower.

THE AMOUNT OF WATER USED PER DAY IS FOR US ONLY AND HAS NOT TAKEN INTO ACCOUNT FOR WATERING OF THE GARDEN, AS THE AMOUNT OF WATER THE GARDEN NEEDS VARIES DEPENDING ON SEASONS AND RAINFALL.

WATER TOWER

one day would come in handy.

leave the heart
of lettuce untouched

Harvest the lettuce by
simply removing the outer
leaves, so that it will
keep producing
new leaves.

Regrowing
apricot
from seed.

How to
regrow pak choi

1 Keep 2 inches
of base

2. stand base
in water

3. change water often

She showed us the secrets

Regrowing green
onions in water.

Always remember to keep the soil
and earthworms healthy by
feeding them with fish and
vegetable scraps. Happy worms
mean healthy soil. Healthy
soil produces
great crops.

4. Once roots are
established, transfer
and replant in soil.

to keep the garden growing.

STEPS TO CATCHING A FISH:

1. BAIT THE HOOK
2. DROP THE LINE INTO THE WATER
3. WHEN YOU FEEL A BITE, GIVE IT A
   TUG AND PULL THE FISH IN.
REMEMBER: PATIENCE IS THE KEY TO CATCHING A FISH.

HEAD: GOOD FOR
STOCK AND SOUP

GUTS: GOOD FOR BAIT FOR THE NEXT CATCH.
ALSO PERFECT AS GARDEN FERTILISER

Simple fishing rod made from a branch and rope.
* Fishing rod not drawn to scale.

We learnt how to fish.

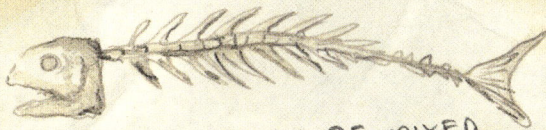

LEFTOVER BONES CAN BE MIXED
WITH OFF-CUT MEATS AND
GROUND UP TO MAKE FISH CAKE.

BONES ARE ALSO WELL
SUITED FOR GARDEN SOIL
AS THEY CAN BE BROKEN DOWN
INTO PLANT FOOD: NITROGEN,
PHOSPHORUS AND CALCIUM.

SKIN: SALTED AND CURED.
MAKES GREAT SNACK.

PACIFIC CHUB MACKEREL
(Scomber japonicus)

TAIL:
SALTED, CURED IN THE SUN.
CAN BE KEPT FOR MANY MONTHS,
ESPECIALLY IN WINTER WHEN
FRESH FISH IS HARD TO FIND.

Hook carved from wood.

How to use every part of the fish
so nothing would go to waste.

NEW WOODEN PLANKS
SALVAGED FROM THE
WATER ARE USED TO FIX
UP DAMAGE FROM
THE STORM.

FIREWOOD
STORAGE

HOME
SWEET
HOME

OUTDOOR
COOKING AREA

VIEW FROM ABOVE

CABIN

WATER TANK

VEGGIE PATCH

MAPLE TREE

APRICOT
TREE

How to make a more comfortable

OLD BARREL FOR
COLLECTING RAINWATER

STOVE MADE FROM
EMPTY STEEL BARREL

DINING
TABLE

SHELF FOR
CD STORAGE

MATTRESS

HAMMOCK

CROSS- SECTION OF OUR
NEW HOME (SHED)

and cosy home for ourselves.

How to keep our dreams afloat.

We smiled.

We laughed.

Her teachings made the days a little less sad.
They gave us strength.

They kept us moving forward.

4.

The
Garden

The fruits were turning ripe.

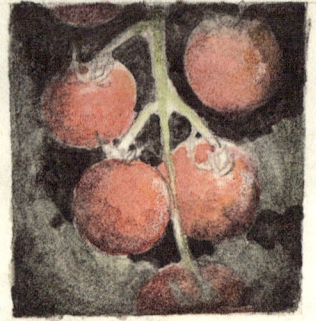

The vegetables that we planted
were ready to be picked.

All across the garden, everything blossomed.

I picked the ripest apricots from the tree
and gave one to my sister. We took a bite.

It tasted delicious.
Grandma's garden had been kind to us.

5.

The
Notebook

TUESDAY:
I saw a narwhal
today. He looks like
my brother

my magical raft
to dry land

The water also brought us many things.

Things that once belonged to others.
Now left behind.

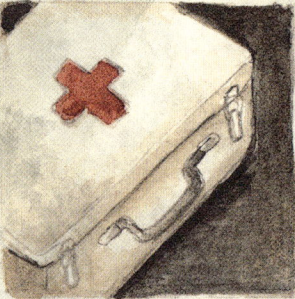

We took only those that we needed to survive.

Hidden in a briefcase, my sister discovered
a notebook, ragged and worn.

The pages were mostly empty, except for
a few that had been filled with drawings.

Drawings of people. Familiar faces. Streets.

Our neighbourhood.
Drawings of life before the flood.

TERU TERU
BŌZU

SHINE
SHINE
MONK

Grandma said all you really
need to make the perfect
apricot jam are:
* Fresh apricots
* sugar
* lemon juice
* and lots of love

STORE IN A COOL, DRY PLACE (OUR CABIN!)
CAN BE KEPT FOR UP TO 2 YEARS!

The notebook became my sister's treasured journal.
She wrote about days on the rooftop garden.

LESSON 34 ☆ ☆ ☆

IT'S GARLIC PLANTING DAY!
(I HATE GARLIC)

Tuesday

TODAY, GRANDMA SHOWED ME HOW TO MAKE A TERU TERU BŌZU, WHICH IS JAPANESE FOR SHINE SHINE MONK. SHE SAID IT HAS MAGICAL POWERS TO BRING GOOD WEATHER AND CHASE THE STORM AWAY.

ON THE 14th DAY, LITTLE LEAVES POP THROUGH THE SOIL. THEY LOOK SO CUTE!

BY THE 20th DAY, MORE GARLIC EMERGES!

* GARLIC LOVES:
  SUN
  WELL-DRAINED SOIL
  MANURE

* GARLIC HATES!
  DRY SOIL
  WEEDS.

Sunday

I saw a weird-looking fish this afternoon. It jumped out of the water like an acrobat. It had blue, yellow, green and red dots. It was an amazing sight. Grandma said it was a mahi-mahi. My brother thought it had a

MAHI-MAHI   funny name

She filled the pages with the lessons Grandma taught us, so that she could one day master those skills too.

DAY
190

6.

Life
Goes On

Every morning, Grandma was up early,
working in the garden.

She sowed new seeds and weeded out the bad ones.

She believed that by nurturing the garden

with love and great care, it would continue

to provide us with all that it could offer.

My daily task was to check how much the
water had risen. Climbing down the fire escape on
the side of the building, I marked the wall.

The water never receded.
It just kept rising with each passing day.

My sister added a tally mark to count the number
of days we had been up on the rooftop. 197 days.

In the afternoon, I fished. I used the guts from the
previous catch as bait. It smelt horrible.

But it was the only thing that attracted the fish.

Most of the time, I caught small fish.
Enough for just the three of us.

But sometimes if I was lucky enough ...

I might catch a BIG one.

Each night, as the day began to lose
its light, we helped Grandma prepare dinner.

The meal was simple.

But what mattered was the feeling of togetherness.

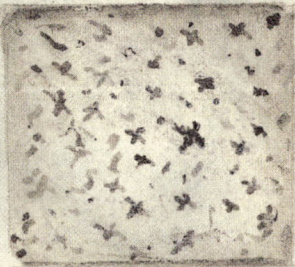

After dinner, we listened to Grandma's stories.

Then, I blew out the candle.

7.

The City

The abandoned city became a home for marine life.

Seagrass grew.

Coral flourished.

Fish thrived.

We caught glimpses of the
world below the water's surface.

Streets bustling with schools of fish.
Jellyfish drifting by like balloons in the sky.

New aquatic tenants filled up the empty apartments.
Our old way of life …

At night, the sea lit up
with a soft, shimmering glow.

It was magical.

The whales sang their sweet lullaby.

We counted the stars, and Grandma reminded
us of how beautiful life could be.

8.

*Harvest
Moon*

The leaves of the deciduous
trees began to change their colours ...

from luscious green to crimson,
orange, yellow and gold.

The warm, summery breeze

was slowly replaced by the cold, blustery wind.

Winter was approaching.

Grandma kept a watchful eye for the time
when the moon was full and big after sunset.

That was when we started to harvest
our crops for the long winter months ahead.

Grandma told us this harvesting was a tradition
that ran in her family when they were living on a farm.

We canned and pickled our harvest.

We salted and cured our last catch of fish.

My sister kept marking the days.

9.

Days
Gone By

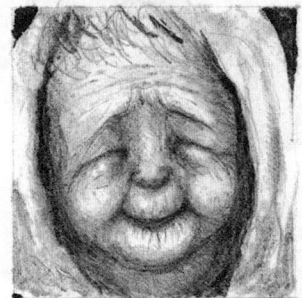

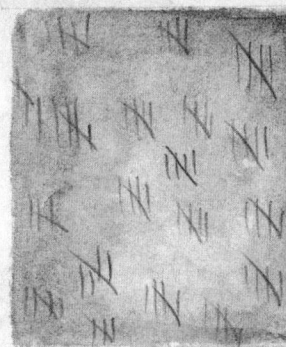

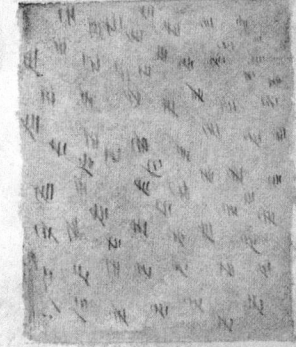

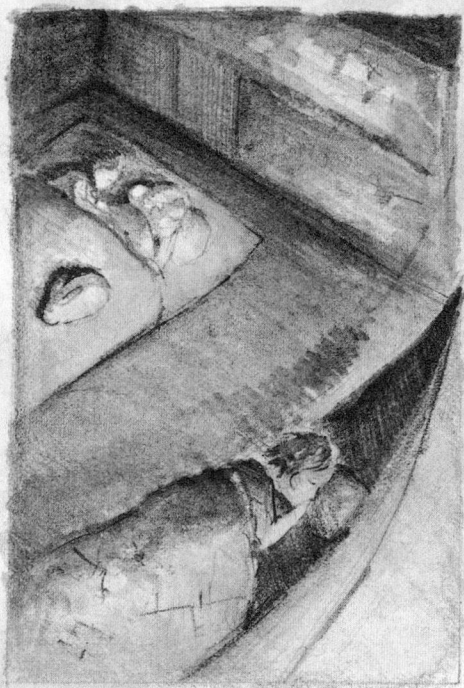

10.

The
Raft

Grandma was becoming weaker.

I took care of the garden so that she could rest.

I sowed new seeds and weeded out the bad ones.

I did everything that I had been taught.

I passed on my knowledge to my sister.

As the seasons came and went,
the storms grew stronger and more hostile.

For months, all it did was rain
with no sign of stopping.

Day by day, the water level rose
higher and higher.

Soon the garden would be underwater.

We built a raft from anything that we could find.

I showed my sister how to tie the ends of the raft
together and make sure the knots were secure.

We showed Grandma the raft.
It wasn't perfect. But it made her proud.

We loaded the raft.

Grandma sat us down beside her underneath the apricot tree. She told us that everything has a purpose.

The garden provided us with gifts, more than we could ever wish for. The garden kept us fed. It kept us safe.

Now the time had come for her to protect
the garden. To watch over it.

My sister cried. I cried.

Grandma said that with each ending,
a new beginning unfolds. Embrace it.

Grandma gave her locket necklace to my
sister. Inside was a photo of the three of us.

She said she would always be with us. Be the light to guide the way. Be the strength to lift us up.

Grandma wrapped her arms around us and kissed us goodbye. It felt as if the world was crashing down.

But we had to carry on. I had to be strong.
I held my sister close and tight as the raft floated
us out into the open water.

I took one last look at the one I loved.
At the place that was once our home.

11.

The
Journey

Setting sail, we drifted off in search of a new home.
We passed our neighbourhood and familiar places.

Along the deserted roads.

Out to sea towards the unknown horizon.

I tried basing my navigation on the Sun and stars.
But it proved useless as I knew nothing about them.

My attempts turned into frustration.
Since there was no way of knowing where to go,

my sister said why not let the winds
and the currents take us instead.

After all, everything would
eventually find its way to shore.

We spent the early hours of the mornings
tending to our edible garden,

making sure our plants were
healthy and well.

We inspected the raft to make sure that the knots
remained tight and secure at all times.

My sister's knots were much better than mine.

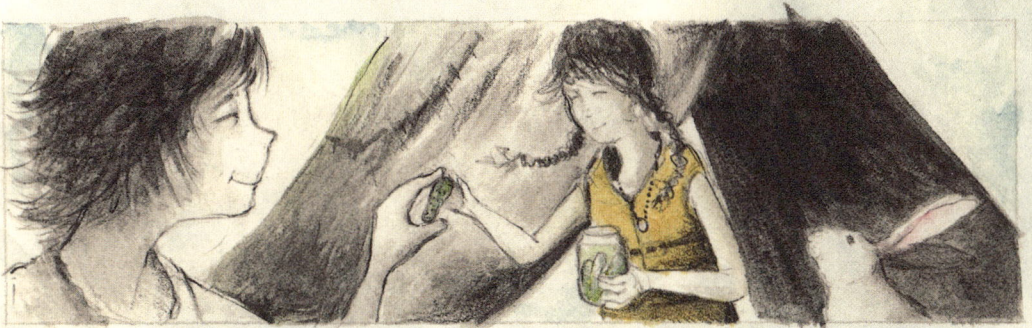

We shared our pickled vegetables.

12.

Lost

It must have been weeks or even longer.
As far as I could see, there was still no land in sight.

I watched the blue sky being
swallowed by the dark, unforgiving clouds.

The storm brewed. The wind blew.
The sea continued to rise.

Thunder growled deep and loud.

It knocked us off our feet.
The pouring rain soaked us to the bone.

We held on to each other. I wished for a miracle.

The sea built itself up like a towering wall of concrete.

Then the tidal wave came tumbling down with
sheer force and drowned us deep below the water.

Exhausted. Defeated. The storm had taken
all that was us. Hope. Spirit.

I felt I had failed my sister and my grandma.
I broke down and cried.

My sister sat beside me.
Her hand rested on my lap.

'Never lose hope,' she whispered.

13.

Beyond
the Horizon

Lost in the waves of a vast, endless sea, we caught
sight of a giant seabird soaring high in the sky.

Its plumage reminded us of
Grandma's speckled dress.

Its presence brought us strength.

We followed it for many days and many nights.

Soft wind gently blew. It raised our spirits.
To push on just a little more.

And when we least expected it, there it was.

In the far distance, treetops began
to emerge from the water.

Power lines.

Rooftops.

We anchored our raft
and climbed the moss-covered hill …

to a new beginning.

It seemed like many moons ago since we
heard voices and laughter and saw faces of people.

To be living among others once again felt like a dream.

The journey led us to a new home. To people we had never met before. But they welcomed us with open arms.

The journey also reunited us with people
we used to know before the flood.
Our neighbours. Our long-lost friends.
Our new family.

Grandma said to never lose hope.
And she was right.

There must be others still out there.

Like we were. Lost. Stranded.

Don't give up.

Acknowledgements

What began as a modest 32-page picture book would soon reshape into a much larger project way beyond what I initially had envisioned. For a number of years, the story underwent many significant changes and rewrites, before being shelved away during the global pandemic when everything slowed down. But it eventually found a home a year after the world opened up. As I write down these acknowledgements, I only begin to realise that seven years have passed from the time that I wrote the first draft.

I owe tremendous thanks to these wonderful people who helped turn this project into a reality.

My sincere gratitude to my publisher, Sophia Whitfield, for believing in this book. Thank you to my designer, Verity Clark, for bringing the book to life with her craft and talent, and for seeing the potential in this project. To my editor, Tasha Evans, for her patience with my countless revisions, and for her guidance in shaping up and rebuilding the story. And thank you to everyone at New Frontier Publishing for embarking on this journey with me and making this book possible. Thank you all from the bottom of my heart.

Thank you to Ana Vivas for her invaluable feedback and encouragement much earlier on. I am grateful to Nancy Conescu for her insights, conversations and pieces of advice back when the story was still far from being decent. Zeno Sworder, thank you for inspiring me with the book recommendation, *Walden* by Henry David Thoreau.

To Evan Laughlin, I will forever cherish our odd hour conversations about all things on life: struggle, solace, acceptance, new beginnings and hope. Their meanings became the foundation for the book. Sleep well, my old friend.

To my mum and sister for their support even when we are continents apart. Thank you to my late dad, who did not live to see the book in its printed form – his teachings hold dear to my heart, always.

Above all, I owe every page of this book to Ari, who is my driving force, guidance and inspiration. *'Take what you have learnt and teach the children of your own'* – this book is for you, son.

Medium Used

The illustrations were done using a combination of watercolour, graphite powder, gouache and acrylic paints.

The cover of the book was put together using traditional methods of paper and mixed media collages.

About Tull

Tull Suwannakit is an author and illustrator of books for children. He is a graduate of Savannah College of Art and Design in Savannah, Georgia, and has illustrated and written numerous children's picture books that have been translated into many languages throughout the world. His publishing clients include New Frontier Publishing, Walker Books, Candlewick Press and Scholastic Press. Working predominantly with watercolour and graphite, Tull's books have been featured in *The Sydney Morning Herald* and *The New York Times* and on ABC's Mornings radio and *Play School* on ABC Kids. Some of his books were included among the Notables list as part of The Children's Book Council of Australia Awards and shortlisted for the Speech Pathology Australia Book of the Year Awards and The Crystal Kite Awards.

Along with his bookmaking, Tull is an art teacher and uses his experience in visual arts and storytelling to promote creative expression for people of all ages. He lives a quiet life with his son and their dog in a rural town nestled among the trees and nature outside Melbourne.

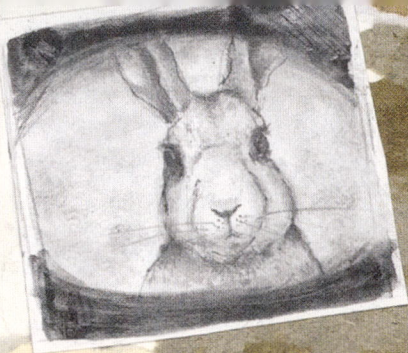

DAY 17

HOME

HOPE